Explorers of the South Pacific

EXPLORATION AND DISCOVERY

EXPLORATION
AND DISCOVERY

Explorers of the South Pacific

A thousand years of exploration, from the
Polynesians to Captain Cook and beyond

Daniel E. Harmon

Mason Crest Publishers
Philadelphia

Mason Crest Publishers
370 Reed Road
Broomall PA 19008

Mason Crest Publishers' world wide web address is
www.masoncrest.com

First printing

1 3 5 7 9 8 6 4 2

Library of Congress Cataloging-in-Publication Data
on file at the Library of Congress

ISBN 1-59084-057-7

EXPLORATION AND DISCOVERY

Contents

Mutiny on the *Bounty*

IT WAS HISTORY'S most famous *mutiny*. In April 1789, the first mate of the British ship H.M.S. *Bounty* led a rebellion that seized the captain and took command of the vessel in the middle of the South Pacific Ocean.

The *Bounty* was sailing from Tahiti, where its crew had gathered a cargo of **breadfruit** plants. They were supposed to transport the breadfruit to the West Indies, off the eastern coast of the Americas. The British government wanted to grow this valuable food crop for its colonies in the West Indies. However, many of the *Bounty*'s sailors had not wanted to leave Tahiti. During their five months there, they had fallen in love with native women. Some had taken

Polynesian wives. They were furious when their comman-
der, Lieutenant William Bligh, forced them to leave.

The mutineers decided not to kill the captain. Instead,
they put Bligh and 18 loyal crewmembers into an open boat
with a small supply of food and water and a few *nautical*
charts. Then they turned the *Bounty* about and returned to
the magical island.

It was a disaster for the rebels. Through dishonest deal-
ings, they made enemies of the once-friendly Tahitian chief.
With some native men and women, they sailed to a distant
island called Tubuai, hoping to settle down for the rest of
their lives. Things soon became worse there than on Tahiti,
however. The Englishmen stole food and women from the
natives and soon found themselves waging an all-out war.

**William Bligh, captain of the
Bounty, was no stranger to
the South Pacific. He had
sailed with Captain James
Cook, the greatest explorer of
the Pacific, and had been
praised by Cook as a skilled
navigator and chartmaker.**

Eventually, a few of the *Bounty* crew and Tahitians sailed to Pitcairn Island, one of the most isolated specks of land in the South Pacific. They took everything ashore and burned the ship. None ever returned to Europe. Some were killed fighting one another; others died of natural causes. Today, about 60 of their descendants inhabit lonely Pitcairn Island.

Lieutenant Bligh, meanwhile, performed one of the most astonishing feats of seafaring history. He successfully steered the ship's boat some 3,500 miles westward to a European settlement on the island of Timor. Extremely weakened and on the brink of death after their long journey over the sun-blistered ocean, they were finally rescued.

If you visit the South Pacific today, you will easily understand why the *Bounty* mutineers did not want to leave Tahiti. To them—and to countless other sailors, explorers, traders, and tourists—it truly was a paradise on earth.

The Pacific is the world's largest ocean. It's little wonder that it took European sea captains almost four centuries to fully explore its southern islands. Even today, scientists learn incredible and sometimes puzzling new things about these remote places, their people, and their wildlife.

Despite the islands' beauty, some of the things the early white explorers saw filled them with disgust. They saw **cannibals** eating human flesh and offering people as sacrifices to native gods. They saw islanders covered with remarkable tattoos—an art form handed down by their ancestors. They saw strange practices of witchcraft.

In the Fiji islands, Robert Quinton, a sea captain who spent much time in the South Pacific a century ago, watched native priests demonstrate "fire walking." The tribe built a great fire over a bed of stones, then cleared away the ashes. Ten dancers in bare feet then began an astonishing ceremony. "Starting in single file, they walked slowly and measuredly across the red-hot stones, chanting in a low monotone," Quinton wrote. "They walked backwards and forwards in the glowing heat, showing not the slightest evidence of inconvenience. The performers remained in the pit for about 10 minutes and then marched out. The doubters examined their feet carefully, but were obliged to admit that they were perfectly normal."

The Pacific Ocean is dotted with clusters of **volcanic islands**. Most of the volcanoes are no longer active. Some islands are populated; some are famous tourist resorts; some have no human inhabitants at all. Most are so small they are practically invisible on many globes. In all, there are approximately 25,000 Pacific islands. The Republic of Fiji has more than 400. Hawaii—a state of the U.S.—has 132. The Philippines encompass some 7,000 islands! Many Pacific islands, like romantic Hawaii and fabled Tahiti, rose from the ocean depths to break the surface millions of years ago.

Scientists believe others, like New Zealand, were parts of a low-lying continent that was flooded when the sea level rose.

Scientists have defined three regions of the South and Central Pacific, with three groups of people. Polynesia is the most widespread area, ranging from Hawaii to Easter Island and southwestward to New Zealand. Its people are known for their beauty and health, as well as for their friendliness.

Melanesia includes New Guinea, the Solomon Islands, and other islands between the Solomons and Fiji. While the Polynesians are noted for their cultural similarities despite the distance between islands, the Melanesians are noted for their many differences. Some 1,200 languages, for example, are spoken on the Melanesian islands.

North of Melanesia is Micronesia, which includes the Caroline, Gilbert, and other islands lying between Hawaii and the Philippines. Like the Polynesians, the Micronesians are interesting because of their similarities. Most of Micronesia lies north of the *equator*.

This book will look back in history at the explorers who found, charted, and settled the South Pacific islands. It begins with the amazing Polynesians and ends with the latter-day European navigators who mapped the last remote islands to be discovered and probed all the way southward to Antarctica.

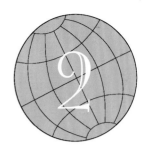

The Polynesians

THE EARLY PEOPLE OF Australia and New Guinea, called *aborigines*, went to sea on crude rafts. Then, they began making canoes out of tree bark. They used sticks—or their hands—as paddles. Very lightweight, these early canoes rode over high ocean waves without being swamped.

Among the greatest ancient navigators were the Polynesians. Scientists are uncertain which island, island group, or continent was the Polynesians' original home. They have Oriental features in appearance, suggesting Asian ties, but they also resemble native peoples of South America and have certain similar customs. This led 20th-century explorer and scientist Thor Heyerdahl to believe

13

they may have **migrated** westward across the Pacific from South America, rather than eastward from the Asian or Australian mainlands.

To prove his theory, in 1947 Heyerdahl set out from Peru with five companions in a crude raft. If they could cross the Pacific safely to the islands of Polynesia using only sail power, it would prove ancient sailors could have done the same—an idea most scientists thought preposterous because of the distances.

Heyerdahl's raft, named Kon-Tiki, was made of large, light balsa logs from the jungle of Ecuador. He and his men lashed the logs together using hemp, a rough form of rope similar to what early Native Americans might have used centuries ago. Heyerdahl refused to use metal bands or nails. He insisted on using only materials that would have been available to South Pacific seafarers many centuries before. They built a breezy deck cabin of bamboo and mounted a large, square sail on a mast.

Amazingly enough, they made it to the Tuamotu Islands near Tahiti—some 4,000 miles away—in 101 days. Although the experiment did not prove the Polynesians had come originally from South America, it showed they *could* have.

Among the Polynesians, canoe making became a practiced skill. Directed by a master craftsman of the village,

An 18th-century painting of a canoe used by the native people of the South Pacific. The Polynesians developed sails and outriggers to make their vessels more seaworthy. They also learned how to determine their position at sea using the stars and currents.

groups of workers would begin with a wide tree trunk. They would scoop out the center using stone axes and seashells, leaving a thin-sided hull. To make the sides higher and more seaworthy against the surging ocean waves, they would sew boards, or *strakes*, along the upper edges. To bore holes in the wood, they used shark-tooth drill bits tied to sticks with animal skin cords. The work was both back-breaking and delicate.

If you've ever ridden in a canoe, you know that great care must be taken to keep it from *capsizing*—that is,

turning over in the water. Polynesians faced the same problem, made worse in choppy seas. In time, the islanders discovered they could make a boat more stable by attaching a floating "arm" several feet out from one side. This balanced the boat wonderfully as it zipped over ocean swells. Canoes

Easter Island, a small island in the South Pacific about 2,400 miles west of South America, is famous for these enormous stone heads, some of which are 65 feet tall and weigh over 50 tons. They were carved about 1,000 years ago by Polynesians who landed on the island in the distant past. Easter Island got its name from the Dutch sailor Jacob Roggeveen, who landed there on Easter Sunday 1722. The Polynesians migrated throughout the South Pacific between 1000 B.C. and A.D. 1000.

made in this way are called *outriggers*.

Polynesian sailors also came to realize they could use the wind to help their canoes go. They learned to harness the wind by raising a pole from the bottom of the raft, tying a crosspiece at the top, and hanging an animal hide or woven

These Polynesian ornaments and figures have been carved from bone. The aborigines of Australia and the Polynesian islanders of the South Pacific lived in isolation until the arrival of European explorers during the 16th and 17th centuries.

mat from it. They worked these simple sails using ropes made of braided coconut fiber. In fair winds, they could sail 100 miles or farther in a day.

The Polynesians in their outrigger canoes ventured great distances across the Pacific. Sometimes they followed birds in flight. They learned natural skills of *navigation*, finding their location from the position of the sun, moon, and constellations. They understood the Pacific's wind patterns and currents, and used them to their advantage.

Their seafaring instincts steadily increased over the centuries. While sailing the open sea, for example, they could tell when they approached land by the look of the clouds and the scent of flowers and other wildlife on the breeze. By sailing in expeditions of many outriggers spread across miles of ocean, the Polynesians increased their likelihood of sighting one of the small, far-flung islands of the vast Pacific.

Over the centuries, Polynesian canoes were made larger and larger. The natives began connecting two large canoes side-by-side, with a platform across the middle. By building a small hut on these planks, they could shelter themselves from the weather. Thus, they created some of the first "ships" in the world. Some of these vessels were longer than a modern house.

Eventually, Polynesian culture spread throughout the South Pacific, from Easter Island off the South American coast to New Zealand in the west and Hawaii in the north, above the equator. Those islands, with Tahiti near the center, are the three corners of the Polynesian "triangle." However, some historians think the Polynesians also sailed the Indian Ocean and possibly reached westward to the coast of Africa.

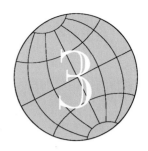

Ferdinand Magellan was a tough Portuguese sailor. After he was dismissed from Portugal's navy by the king, he moved to Spain, where he planned a journey west across the Atlantic Ocean. It would become one of the greatest sea voyages of exploration.

Ferdinand Magellan

THE LONG VOYAGES of the Polynesians were remarkable because they challenged the ocean and the weather in relatively small, though sturdy, craft. They used the simplest of "charts"—webs fashioned of twigs and seashells—and they did not even have magnetic *compasses*.

By the early 1500s, Europeans were poised to enter Pacific waters. Their instruments were primitive compared to those of modern-day ships and yachts. But compared to the Polynesians, they had "state-of-the-art" tools for finding the course. One of the early European captains, Ferdinand Magellan, was prepared to explore and map the great ocean.

Magellan was born to a wealthy Portuguese family in

King Charles V of Spain was a great supporter of exploration. He wanted to find new lands, because the riches and natural resources of these lands could increase Spain's power and wealth. When Magellan told the king he could find a way for Spain to reach the Far East, Charles was willing to send a small fleet on the search.

1480, but it was not for Portugal that he set forth on his famous round-the-world voyage in search of the Orient. It was for Spain. Although he had sailed and fought for his home country in far-off lands, in 1517 the king of Portugal refused Magellan's request for a fleet to sail westward to the Orient. Magellan then decided to leave Portugal and move to Spain. Two years later, King Charles of Spain sent him to sea in command of five ships. Magellan planned to sail west across the Atlantic, find a passage through the Americas, and proceed west to the Orient. There he would gather a cargo of valuable *spices*, then return to Spain.

Magellan's fleet left Spain in September of 1519. The voyage across the Atlantic and along the coast of South

America was long and demanding. At one stretch, it rained for 60 days, and winds and storms slowed progress. Soon, some of Magellan's officers began voicing discontent and challenging his leadership.

On April Fool's Day 1520, in the darkness and confusion of a storm, 30 officers and sailors mutinied. The rebels captured two of the five ships. Fortunately for Magellan, most of his men remained loyal. They recaptured the ships and punished the mutineers.

A few months later, one of Magellan's ships was wrecked in a gale. It was mid-October 1520 before the remaining vessels reached the entrance to what Magellan hoped would be a **strait**, or sea passage, through the continent. They had been gone from Spain more than a year and were still in the Atlantic Ocean!

Cautiously, Magellan navigated his fleet through the shallow passage. The winds and currents were fierce and unpredictable. At night, the men could see the campfires of hostile natives ashore. Clearly, it would not do to land here unless there was an emergency.

On November 18, 1520, the explorers emerged into the South Pacific—but not before losing a ship to another mutiny. Officers and crewmen had locked the ship's captain in irons and turned the vessel homeward. Magellan and his faithful comrades aboard the other vessels were unaware of

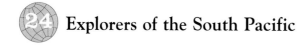

This drawing from a 16th-century book shows Magellan's ships in the South Pacific, surrounded by strange sea creatures. The voyage across the Pacific took much longer than Magellan had expected.

this. For all they knew, the missing ship was lost at sea. Their small fleet was now down to three vessels.

Behind them now were the storms and angry natives of South America. Ahead lay thousands of miles of open ocean. At first, the days and weeks passed peacefully. The crews fished for albacore and bonito. The weather was wonderful, the sea fairly calm.

Magellan did not realize it, however, but he had made a terrible mistake before striking out across the Pacific. He had not taken time to put ashore along South America's west coast for fresh food and, most importantly, drinking water. This was understandable, for Magellan had no idea how vast the Pacific Ocean is. He believed that in no time at all he would be in the Orient, filling his ships' holds with supplies and valuable cargo.

Another decision that would cause grave problems—although again, he did not realize it—was the direction in which he chose to sail. Magellan set a northwesterly course that took his fleet just above some of the southern islands in the middle of the Pacific. Had he found these islands, he could have sent boats ashore for water and food.

Soon, the men became worried because they had not found land. By early 1521, the **mariners** were forced to ration their food and water. With only spoiled food to eat and no fresh vegetables or fruit, they fell sick with **scurvy**. This was an illness common in the early years of long ocean voyages. Without proper vitamins, sailors' bodies—especially their gums and joints—become very sore. The men's mouths became so sore it was painful to eat. They began to die. Only a few were well enough to work the sails.

By February, there was little food to eat. The sailors caught and skinned sharks. They ate the remnants of their

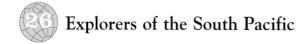

food stores, which had become filthy during many months at sea. Finally, they resorted to cooking and eating leather and even sawdust. The rats that scurried through the ships' holds became a valuable source of meat.

After passing two barren islands and a third where the natives were too hostile for the Spaniards to land, Magellan's three ships reached the island of Samar in March 1521. Samar is part of the Philippines. The first Europeans had crossed the Pacific! Here, they found friendly natives who wished to trade with them. With fresh water and food, the Spaniards soon revived. In awkward gestures and fragmented speech, they began to preach the Christian gospel to the natives. Converting the natives of the Pacific to Christianity was one of the objectives of Magellan's expedition. Thousands of islanders were baptized.

All too soon, however, Magellan stumbled into disaster. Natives on the neighboring islands of Cebu and Mactan began arguing. When their clash turned violent, Magellan felt he should support the people of Cebu, who had befriended him. With 49 men, he invaded Mactan by boat on April 27, 1521. To his horror, he was met by many more warriors than he had expected. After the Spaniards set fire to a village, they were driven to the beach by 1,500 natives. Fighting to board their boats and escape, Magellan and eight other Spaniards fell in the surf, mortally wounded.

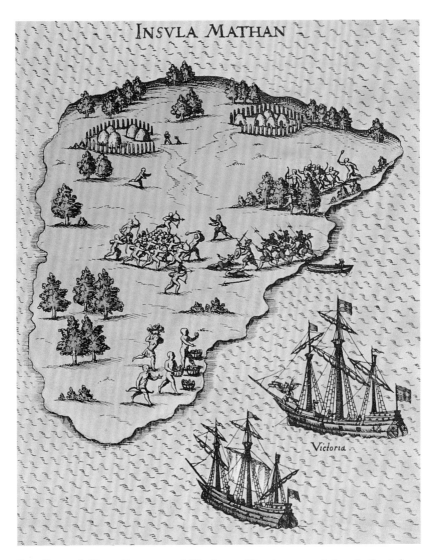

Ferdinand Magellan was killed on Mactan, an island that is part of the Philippines in the South Pacific. He made the mistake of becoming involved in tribal politics.

The Spanish officers watching the battle from the ships did not help Magellan. Some of them disliked their leader, and they did not believe they should be involved in a feud among the islanders. Perhaps they also were afraid.

The *Victoria* was the only one of Magellan's ships to return to Spain. It arrived in September 1522—three years after the voyage had begun. Only 35 members of the original crew of more than 280 sailors ever returned home to Spain.

Magellan's grand mission did not end there, however. After more misadventures among the islands of the western Pacific, his surviving crew lost one of their remaining ships and abandoned another. At last, the lone *Victoria* sailed westward across the Indian Ocean and rounded Africa. The leaky, ragged-sailed *Victoria* arrived in Seville, Spain, on September 8, 1522. Only 35 Spaniards (including some who made their way home after the *Victoria* landed) survived the first round-the-world voyage, which took almost three years. But the cargo of spice brought from the Orient by that single ship more than paid for the expedition—in terms of money, at least. In terms of lost lives, it had been a horrible ordeal.

Magellan's expedition had proved the Orient indeed could be reached by sailing west from Europe. Was it the best route? That remained to be seen. And as the *Victoria*'s log revealed, there was much ocean to be explored between the Americas and the Far East.

The Solomon Islands were discovered by a Spanish explorer named Alvaro de Mendaña de Neira. However, Mendaña believed that the Solomons were part of a southern continent. This was a common problem in the exploration of the South Pacific. Until exact maps were drawn in the 18th century, sailors could never be certain whether the lands they saw were separate islands or connected to a larger land mass.

Mendaña and Quirós

MORE SPANISH AND Portuguese sailors entered the South Seas throughout the 1500s. The Europeans were competing fiercely to set up trading posts in the East Indies (present-day Indonesia), New Guinea, and other islands in the South Pacific. By the mid-1500s, they had a new reason to probe the remote reaches of the ocean. They had heard of a large island, possibly a continent, far to the south. Two men who went looking for this land were Alvaro de Mendaña de Neira and his pilot, Pedro Fernandez de Quirós.

In 1567–68, Mendaña made his first voyage into the South Pacific. Sailing from a Spanish-held seaport in Peru on the South American coast, he discovered a number of

Pacific islands previously unknown to Europeans. These included the Solomons, east of New Guinea. He believed—incorrectly, as it turned out—that the Solomon Islands were part of the legendary "southern continent."

The expedition encountered the Pacific in all its dark tempers: parching heat, contrary winds that made progress difficult and at times impossible . . . and storms. On the return trip, a *typhoon* slammed the fleet. It capsized one ship, and the crew could right it only after cutting off the main mast, sails, and lines. When the tempest blew past, they fashioned a small sail and eventually arrived at the North American coast.

Like Magellan, Mendaña was eager to meet Pacific islanders. He admired the colorful costume of a chief called Bilebanara and the natives' dancing and music. However, the Spaniards were shocked by some of their hosts' customs. One tribe of cannibals offered human food to the Spaniards! Appalled, Mendaña's men buried the flesh.

To the disappointment of the Spanish government, however, Mendaña brought home little of value. It was 1595—almost 30 years later—before Mendaña finally set forth on his second expedition. This time, he took with him Quirós, a young but capable navigator. Mendaña's six ships carried more than 600 soldiers and hopeful settlers, including his wife and other relatives. Mendaña intended to become governor of the new land.

They did not reach their earlier landfall in the Solomon Islands. Instead, they put ashore at the Santa Cruz Islands, several hundred miles to the east, and started a settlement. The islanders were friendly—but the Spaniards were not. They killed some of the natives, including a chief.

Soon, the Spaniards were quarreling among themselves. Some did not like the way Mendaña was running the settlement. They were low on food. Those who opposed Mendaña spread fear and discontent. They insisted that Mendaña let them return home. He refused and ordered his loyal soldiers to kill the leader of the troublemakers.

However, their problems were only beginning. A deadly disease broke out. Many Spaniards died—including Mendaña and his brother-in-law. The natives, furious at the treatment the newcomers had given them, loomed menacingly nearby.

It was clear now the survivors would have to leave. They pleaded with Mendaña's widow, governess of the ill-fated colony, to abandon the settlement. She agreed. On Quirós fell the burden of getting them to safety.

They set a course for the Spanish port of Manila in the Philippine Islands—more than 3,000 miles to the northwest. Some of the weary adventurers were still sick and died at sea. The journey took almost three months. Their supply of drinking water ran dangerously low, and two vessels were lost to storms. The ships by that time were rotting and barely seaworthy. Thanks largely to Quirós' determination and skill as a navigator, the remnants of Mendaña's tragic expedition arrived at Manila in February 1596.

After this, Quirós wanted desperately to renew the search for the "southern continent." To do it, he needed the backing of his government. Quirós had an idea. If he could persuade the Pope in Rome that countless natives in the mysterious southern regions might be converted to Christianity by **missionaries**, the Pope might help him get government support for a new expedition.

It worked. Pope Clement sent a formal recommendation to Spain, urging the king to send Quirós in command of a voyage to find the "Antarctic" land, as the distant continent had come to be known.

Years passed, however, before Quirós could begin his voyage. First, he had to make his way back to South America from Spain. On the voyage across the Atlantic, he was shipwrecked. Finally arriving at Venezuela on the northern coast, he made his way to the western side of the continent. At last, he reached the port of Callao, Peru. There, he organized a small fleet of three ships. His party of more than 100, including six Roman Catholic priests, prepared to sail. It was late December 1605.

After reviewing the plans of Pedro Fernandez de Quirós, Pope Clement asked the king of Spain to send an expedition to the South Pacific. The Catholic king was anxious to please the Pope, and agreed to the request.

A storm drove the ships farther north than Quirós had intended. In six weeks, they were halfway across the ocean at an island group known today as the Low Archipelago. Two months later, they came to another island group, the New Hebrides. Quirós mistakenly thought New Hebrides was the continent Europeans had been searching for, which he called Australia del Espiritu Santo. He staged a grand ceremony on the shore, proclaiming for Spain all the land from there to the South Pole. Little did he realize this was only another of the South Pacific's many islands. Thousands of miles of open water lay between there and the frozen southern continent.

Quirós wanted to build a great city in the New Hebrides and call it New Jerusalem. He sent some soldiers to explore the area—and they quickly got into a deadly squabble with island warriors. In the coming weeks, the Spaniards raided native villages and stole livestock, causing more ill will.

Quirós stayed on the island only a month. Then he set out to chart more of his "continent." The ships were separated by a storm, and their captains were unable to reunite. Quirós returned across the Pacific, landing on the west coast of Mexico.

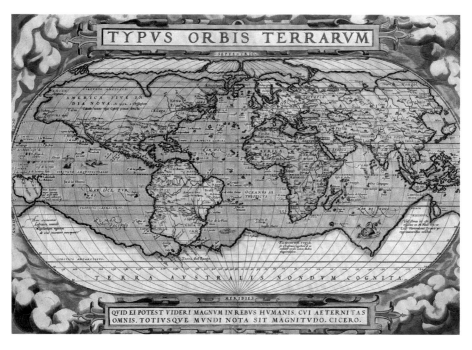

As this map from a late 16th-century atlas shows, geographers of Europe believed there was a large southern continent. On this map the land is called Terra Australis Nondum Cognita—the southern land that has not yet been discovered.

Quirós earned no reward for his efforts back in Spain. He arrived home in late 1607 with hardly enough money to support himself. He was so poor, he had to sell clothes and other personal items to pay for his account of the voyage to be printed. Finally, the king of Spain granted him some money.

Quirós wanted to return to the South Pacific, but the Spanish government stalled. When he finally obtained permission, the year was 1614 and Quirós was near the end of his life. He sailed to Panama, but died there before he could organize another expedition across the Pacific.

Compared to island natives, European sailors were a filthy lot. Cooped aboard ship for months, the visiting mariners stank with body odors. Native Tahitians, by contrast, bathed several times a day in island streams and pools. They used plant oils to clean and perfume their hair and bodies. The women wore fragrant, lovely wildflowers in their hair.

The crews of Mendaña and Quirós had treated the natives badly. On some of the islands, their actions had planted seeds of distrust toward Europeans that would last for centuries to come. However, the two explorers provided detailed early descriptions of the islands they visited and the people they met. Gradually, Europeans were getting an accurate picture of the Pacific world.

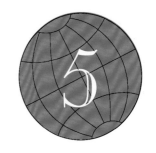

The Dutch and French Explore the Pacific

IN A WAY, Abel Janszoon Tasman was a failure: He set out to explore the Australian coast and missed the continent altogether! However, he did discover New Zealand, 1,200 miles to the southeast, and Tasmania, just off Australia's southern coast.

The story of Australia's original discovery may never be known. Chinese and other Asian peoples probably knew something of the continent as early as A.D. 1300. Several hundred years later, when European explorers and traders began arriving in the region, they had trouble determining which bodies of land were islands and island groups, and which ones might be part of a large continent.

In 1503, a French captain named Binot Paulmyer, sieur de Gonneville, was forced ashore in the southern latitudes. He may have been the first European to land on Australia, but he lost his records, which would have shown his position. Some suspect his ship had been driven onto the coast of Madagascar—all the way across the Indian Ocean. Others think he may have been in the South Atlantic, half a world away from Australia.

Throughout the 1500s, others claimed to have found the continent. In time, most claims were found to be wrong. However, by the mid-1600s, Dutch ship captains trading in the Indian Ocean and Malaysia had sailed along parts of western and southwestern Australia and around the great gulf in the north, known today as the Gulf of Carpenteria.

In 1642, the Dutch East India Company, a great trading organization operating in the Indian Ocean, sent Tasman to the South Pacific. His mission was to discover "the unknown and found Southland, the South East coast of Nova Guinea [New Guinea], together with the islands located thereabout." Tasman sailed east from Mauritius, a Dutch-held island in the Indian Ocean. Steering too far southward, he passed Australia and came to a large island instead. Tasman named the island Van Diemen Land in honor of Anthony van Diemen, governor-general of the Dutch East Indies. Later, it would become known as Tasmania.

More than 1,000 miles farther east, Tasman came to another large island. He named it Staten Island. This was the lower section of modern-day New Zealand.

The expedition veered northeast to the Tonga Islands, then turned westward. Passing the Fiji Islands, Tasman bore to the northwest and skirted the north coast of New Guinea—which he wrongly believed to be part of Australia—before ending his voyage.

In the coming years, European countries sent more adventurers into the South Pacific. Men of all types represented England, from *buccaneer* William Dampier to naval commanders Samuel Wallis (who discovered Tahiti) and Philip Carteret. One of Tasman's fellow Dutchmen, Jacob

After taking a position with the Dutch East India Company in 1632, Abel Tasman spent most of the rest of his life in the South Pacific. After his 1642 voyage, during which he discovered Tasmania and New Zealand, Tasman made a second voyage in 1644. During this trip, he charted the coast of New Guinea and Australia.

Roggeveen, discovered the Society Islands, mysterious Easter Island with its ancient stone statues and carvings of "bird men," and Samoa in the 1720s.

The first Frenchman to sail around the world was Louis-Antoine Comte de Bougainville. He served with the French army in North America during the mid-1700s before turning his energy to seafaring. During the 1760s, Bougainville established a French colony at the Falkland Islands in the South Atlantic. When his king gave up the Falklands to Spanish rivals, Bougainville decided to sail around the world. In the autumn of 1766, he set out in two ships, taking along scientists to study the places and wildlife he would find.

Visiting Tahiti, Bougainville was impressed by the natives' friendly welcome and flowery ceremonies. Bougainville's only complaint was that they took from the visitors whatever caught their eye. To the Tahitians, this wasn't exactly stealing, and they did not mean to anger the Frenchmen.

On one occasion, an aging islander came aboard the ship to offer his three daughters as wives to the French. Bougainville thanked him, but refused. After the man and his daughters left, Bougainville noticed that one of his important navigational instruments was missing. He sent crewmen in a boat to catch the natives. When the elderly

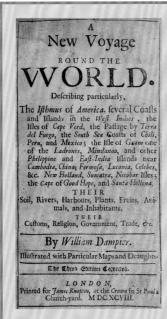

In the 17th century, an Englishman named William Dampier rekindled interest in exploring the South Pacific. Dampier was a pirate who made his fortune raiding Spanish settlements on the west coast of South America in 1679. He then sailed west across the Pacific to Australia, and continued on around the world. In 1697 Dampier wrote a book about his adventures in the South Pacific. It became very popular and inspired many voyages.

man saw them coming, he willingly paddled toward them and gave back the instrument. He had not realized it was something the captain needed and thought it would be all right to take it.

From Tahiti, Bougainville sailed west to Samoa, then on to the New Hebrides. At times, he faced some of the same dangers as Europeans who had come before him had: dwindling food supplies and the spread of scurvy among his crew. They were relieved finally to see the coast of Australia. Turning north, they sailed to New Britain, then westerly along the upper coast of New Guinea. Reaching the Dutch settlements, they received much-needed rest, treatment for their sicknesses, and food.

Despite more than 250 years of European exploration, until the late 18th century much of the South Pacific remained unknown. That changed because of an English captain named James Cook, who made three voyages through the Pacific and created maps that were so accurate they could still be used today.

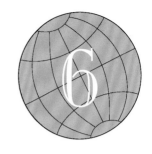

The Voyages of Captain Cook

ALTHOUGH BY THE 18th century a southern continent had still never been found in the Pacific Ocean, many geographers of the time were convinced that it existed. In the late 18th century, the Royal Society, an organization of scientists in Great Britain, developed a plan to find the continent. The Society would work with the British Navy, sending a ship west across the South Pacific between the latitudes of 35 and 40 degrees. Within this strip of the globe, the British believed, lay the fabled continent. Latitude 40 degrees south is the imaginary line that passes west-east just below Australia, through the North Island of New Zealand, and—half a world away in South America—

through Chile and Argentina. The leader of this voyage would be a respected navy captain named James Cook.

Once he discovered the continent, Cook was to carefully chart its coast, noting the water depths and currents. He was to bring back samples of interesting plants and minerals. He was to befriend any natives he found, if possible, and trade with them. And, naturally, he was to claim the continent for England.

Cooke did not find Terra Australis. Rather, he sailed all the way to New Zealand in a **bark** called *Endeavour*. He charted its coast, then proceeded to Australia, reaching the continent in April 1770. Cook sailed up the east coast, again making careful notes for pilots who would come later.

Cruising near the northeastern tip of Australia one night, the *Endeavour* suddenly crunched onto the Great Barrier Reef. This is a long formation of coral just at the surface of the waves. The crew had to throw guns and heavy supplies overboard to make the ship light enough to float off. The *Endeavour* was stuck on the reef until high tide the next night. The reef had punched a hole in the bottom of the ship. To close it, the crew spread a spare sail across the bottom of the *Endeavour*.

Not long afterward, a strong tide again pushed the ship toward the foaming breakers of the Great Barrier Reef. There was no wind—which meant Cook could not use sail

The Early Life of Captain Cook

Born in 1728, James Cook was working as a grocer's apprentice as a boy. He decided he wanted to spend his life on the water, not on land, so at age 17 he signed aboard a coal-carrying ship as a seaman. Later, he joined the Royal Navy—again, as a ordinary sailor. His greatest strength was that he understood the sea and sailors rather than international politics. He took care, for example, to see that his men ate proper foods aboard ship. This, he proved, could prevent dangerous scurvy outbreaks.

After a short time as a common seaman, Cook's knowledge and talents were obvious to his superiors. He was made a ship's master and soon was given command of a British ship of war.

In 1768, the English government appointed him to command a ship called *Endeavour*. His mission: to find the "southern continent," Terra Australis, which other mariners had tried for 200 years to locate.

power to turn away from the dangerous coral rocks. He ordered men to lower boats, tie ropes to the ship, and try to pull it out of harm's way by rowing. However, they were not strong enough to beat the force of the current.

Fortunately, just before the ship crashed, a lookout sighted a narrow opening in the sharp rocks. With the rowers laboring furiously, Cook steered toward the opening. It did

Cook's men raise the British flag in Australia in the spring of 1770. With his voyages through the South Pacific, Cook forever disproved the theory that a large continent existed to the south of Australia.

not seem they would make it in time. Then, an unexpected breeze came up. With the added power of its sails, the *Endeavour* reached the opening in the reef and passed safely through.

Cook returned home in 1771 and made his valuable report to the admiralty. In July 1772, he sailed from Plymouth, England, on his second voyage to the South Seas. This time, he went to the Cape of Good Hope at the bottom of Africa, continued south to about 60 degrees latitude, and began circling the globe from west to east. He found plenty of icebergs, but no sign of Terra Australis. His reports did add to the growing body of knowledge about the southern seas, however. He spent much time exploring little-known island groups.

Tahiti he found to be an island paradise—but not always a peaceful one. At one point, Cook was caught in the middle of a native civil war. In April 1774, he watched a massive fleet of more than 300 Polynesian craft, including many twin-hulled battle canoes and some 7,000 warriors, gather at Tahiti to attack the nearby island of Moorea.

When Cook stopped at Easter Island in 1774, he found a land of fear. A tribe of warriors called Matatoa terrorized the other islanders. They apparently were cannibals who ate human flesh and made human sacrifices. The Matatoa raided peaceful clans who lived in caves, carrying away their victims and torturing them. The English stayed at Easter Island only a few days.

Cook began his third Pacific voyage in 1776. He visited more islands and spent several months at Tahiti. Cook loved Tahiti and its people. On one occasion, he saw a play performed by Polynesians in colorful costumes. Then he sailed northward. In January 1778, he saw the Hawaiian Islands while on the way to Alaska, where he probed the Bering Strait, which separates Alaska from Russia. He was fascinated by the people he met in the cold region, who hung beads from their ears and bird feathers from their noses. His men added fresh walrus meat to their *provisions*.

This watercolor painting is believed to be an accurate view of the death of Captain Cook. It was painted by the brother of a man on Cook's third expedition.

Cook decided to return to Hawaii for the winter of 1778–79. His crew welcomed the plan, but it would prove to be tragic. The Hawaiians were delighted to see the Englishmen when they arrived in November 1778. When the ships anchored, thousands of friendly natives swarmed around and crowded aboard. Some came out by canoe; others swam around the scene "like shoals of fish," Cook wrote.

At first, the Hawaiians and English got along well. Cook was treated like a god. Then, feelings turned sour. The natives soon had no more gifts to give their guests. Tensions grew. A few of the islanders began stealing items from the anchored ship. Anger rose on both sides. When the Hawaiians stole a boat the British had left anchored in the bay, Cook went ashore with an armed force to take it back. Alarmed, the natives gathered in an angry mob. They pressed menacingly around the sailors, who tried to withdraw. Clubs and knives were brandished. Cook was struck, drawing blood. When the islanders saw he was only a human, not a god, they attacked furiously. Cook fell into the surf and was mauled to death.

Cook had mixed feelings about the South Pacific and its people. He did not approve of all their customs—especially the human sacrifices. On the other hand, he had to agree with his rowdy sailors that this indeed was a tropical paradise. And he knew it never would be the same after the Europeans arrived. "I often think it would have been better for them," he once wrote, "if we had never appeared among them." As for the "southern continent," Cook believed it existed, but doubted Europeans ever would find and settle it. In his journal on his second voyage, he wrote of "thick fogs, snow storms, intense cold" and other dangers and hardships. "[N]o man will ever venture further than I have done," he predicted. To go further into the gloomy, frigid southern waters, he said, was to risk being trapped in the ice.

He was right about the icy seas—but wrong about the possibility of discovering Antarctica.

In 1911 Roald Amundsen (inset) led a Norwegian expedition to the South Pole. This drawing, made from a photograph, shows Amundsen's assistant Hansen with a sledge and team of huskies. Amundsen won the race to be the first at the South Pole, beating a British team commanded by Robert F. Scott by just a month.

Cracking the Antarctic Ice

DESPITE COOK'S FRUSTRATED prediction, the "southern continent" was discovered not long after his death. It's not clear to historians who first sighted Antarctica, but we know that two explorers saw it at practically the same time. One was a Russian, Fabian Bellingshausen. The other was an Englishman, Edward Bransfield. Both arrived around the coast in January 1820. Bransfield planted the flag of Great Britain on one of the islands, named it New South Britain, and claimed it for King George IV. This was in the South Shetland Islands, just off the Antarctic coast below the tip of South America.

It is interesting that Bransfield landed on Antarctica

during the penguins' breeding season. The island beach was covered with the clumsy animals, whose strange, strong odor was "the most intolerable stench . . . that I ever smelt," he wrote. When sailors rowed ashore to look for fresh drinking water, they had to hack a lane through the mass of angry, beaked inhabitants.

While Bransfield's crewmen were battling penguins, Bellingshausen was nosing around the continent from west to east. Eventually, he, too, arrived at the South Shetlands. There, Bellingshausen met an American seal hunter named Nathanael Palmer. It's possible Palmer, who had been seal-ing in the region for some time, was the actual discoverer of the Antarctic mainland.

Regardless of who first saw it, there was little any of the early explorers could do with the frozen continent. Because of the ice-filled seas, it was difficult just to make a landing. Gradually, however, various expeditions pushed through the ice to examine and claim different parts of the Antarctic coast. One explorer who made important find-ings in the South Seas and Antarctica was Charles Wilkes. From 1838 to 1842, he led the United States Exploring Expedition. Among other accomplishments, they charted part of Antarctica.

Wilkes' ships were not the most seaworthy vessels on the ocean. The idea that they would take on the ice-filled

American naval officer Charles Wilkes was awestruck by the icy waters around Antarctica. He wrote: "Some of the bergs were of magnificent dimensions, one-third of a mile in length, and from 150 to 200 feet in height, with sides perfectly smooth, as though they had been chiseled. Others, again, exhibited lofty arches of many-coloured tints, leading into deep caverns, open to the swell of the sea, which, rushing in, produced loud and distant thunderings. . . . Every noise on board, even our own voices, reverberated from the massive and pure white walls."

waters around Antarctica seemed ridiculous to some observers—and even to some of Wilkes' officers and crew. Nor was the expedition well equipped. When they reached Sydney, Australia, where they spent the first winter, the Americans realized they had no tools with which to cut the thick ice they would certainly encounter.

The expedition sailed southward from Australia, past Tasmania, directly into the ice-choked Antarctic seas. They then made their way westward almost a quarter of the way around the continent before returning to Australia.

During the same time period, the British Royal Navy was examining the continent's coast. Sir James Clark Ross led this expedition. With many years of experience exploring the Arctic north, Ross and his crew were much better prepared than Wilkes for weathering the savage Antarctic climate.

Among other achievements, Ross explored what is known today as the Ross Sea—the southernmost extreme end of the Pacific Ocean. At the latitude where the sea turned to a solid, vast ice shelf, Ross found a large island with two lofty volcanic mountains. He named the peaks Erebus and Terror. How strange it must have been to see fire and smoke belching into the frozen air from the cap of Mount Erebus, surrounded by a domain of grey and white!

A French expedition, meanwhile, was exploring a different part of the Antarctic coast. Other parties from various countries followed. Soon, adventurers were clamoring to cross the ice desert all the way to the South Pole. A Norwegian, Roald Amundsen, became the first human to reach the South Pole in 1911.

By that time, the major islands and landmasses of the South Pacific and Antarctica had been located and defined. But much remained to be learned. Latter-day voyagers like Thor Heyerdahl, for instance, have crossed the Pacific in primitive craft, learning firsthand the ways of the ancient Polynesians and other islanders. Scientists marvel at the awesome remains of early island civilizations, like the stone statues on Easter Island. Permanent scientific stations in Antarctica gather information that tell us not just about the icy continent, but about changes that are taking place in the earth's atmosphere.

To the early European explorers, the South Seas were a world apart, filled with beauty, natural riches, and mystery. Today, the remote islands still beckon visitors for the same reasons.

Chronology

1000 B.C.	The migration of the Polynesian people begins.
A.D. 950	The Maoris settle in New Zealand.
1513	Vasco Núñez de Balboa leads a Spanish expedition across the isthmus of Panama and becomes the first European to see the western shores of the Pacific Ocean.
1519– 1522	Ferdinand Magellan discovers a route through South America and sails across the Pacific Ocean, eventually traveling around the world.
1567	Alvaro de Mendaña de Neira explores the South Pacific, landing on the Solomon Islands.
1571	The Spanish conquer the Philippines, a large group of islands in the South Pacific.
1595	Mendaña sets out on a second expedition, intending to establish a Spanish colony in the Solomon Islands; the Dutch East India Company begins trading in Southeast Asia.
1596	Pedro Fernandez de Quirós brings the survivors of the Mendaña expedition to Manila.
1603	Binot Paulmyer, a French explorer, is blown off course and may have landed on Australia.
1606	The Dutch sailor Willem Jansz reaches Australia.

Chronology

1642	Abel Tasman circles Australia and discovers New Zealand.
1697	William Dampier writes *A New Voyage Around the World*, a description of his adventures in the South Pacific which inspires new voyages of discovery.
1722	Jacob Roggeveen discovers the Society Islands, Easter Island, and Samoa.
1728	James Cook is born.
1766	Bougainville sails for the South Seas with a team of scientists to study the island wildlife.
1768	Captain Cook sets out on his first voyage to the South Pacific.
1770	Cook lands on Australia and explores the coast.
1779	Cook is killed by natives in Hawaii during his third voyage.
1788	The first English settlement is established in Australia.
1861	Robert Burke and William Wills die while trying to cross Australia. The continent will be crossed successfully the next year by John Stuart.
1911	Roald Amundsen reaches the South Pole.

Glossary

aborigine—a person who is the first or earliest known to a region.

bark—a type of sailing ship.

breadfruit—a large round seedless tropical fruit that is usually eaten baked or roasted, when it takes on the texture of bread. The tree that bears breadfruit is native to the Pacific Islands.

buccaneer—a pirate.

cannibal—a person who eats human flesh.

capsize—to overturn on the surface of the water.

compass—a device for finding directions, usually with a magnetic needle that points north.

equator—an imaginary east-west line around the center of the earth.

mariner—a person who sails the oceans.

migrate—to move, either permanently or with changing seasons, from one locale to another.

missionary—somebody sent to another country by a church to spread its faith.

mutiny—a rebellion against legal authority, especially by soldiers or sailors refusing to obey orders and attacking their officers.

nautical—having to do with the oceans and navigation.

Glossary

navigation—the art of steering a vessel.

outrigger—a long float sticking out from the side of a boat, used to prevent it from capsizing.

provisions—supplies needed for a journey, usually food.

scurvy—a disease common among sailors who went on long voyages, caused by poor diets and resulting in weakness and soreness, inflamed gums, and other symptoms.

spice—food flavorings derived from plants, which were very valuable in Europe during the 15th and 16th centuries.

strait—a narrow body of water that joins two larger bodies of water.

strake—a wooden plank used to build up a ship's side.

typhoon—a violent tropical storm.

volcanic island—an island formed by the tops of underwater mountains that are or were active volcanoes.

Further Reading

Gallagher, Jim. *Ferdinand Magellan and the First Voyage Around the World.* Philadelphia: Chelsea House, 2000.

Konstam, Angus. *Historical Atlas of Exploration, 1492–1600.* New York: Checkmark Books, 2000.

MacDonald, Fiona. *Exploring the World.* New York: Bedrick Books, 1999.

Shields, Charles. *James Cook and the Exploration of the Pacific.* Philadelphia: Chelsea House, 2002.

Stefoff, Rebecca. *Scientific Explorers: Travels in Search of Knowledge.* New York: Oxford University Press, 1993.

Internet Resources

The Voyages of Captain Cook

http://www.mariner.org/age/cook.html

http://www.south-pole.com/p0000071.htm

http://pacific.vita.org/pacific/cook/

European exploration in the South Pacific and Antarctic

http://pacific.vita.org/pacific/

http://homepages.ihug.co.nz/~tonyf/

http://www.south-pole.com/p0000052.htm

The Polynesians

http://www.southpacific.org/text/polynesia.html

http://www.wku.edu/~smithch/S131.htm

http://www.pbs.org/wayfinders/polynesian2.html

Index

Photo Credits

About the Author

Daniel E. Harmon of Spartanburg, South Carolina, has written 30 books and numerous articles on topics ranging from history to humor. He is the editor of *The Lawyer's PC*, a national computer newsletter, and associate editor of *Sandlapper: The Magazine of South Carolina*.